LATIN, GREEK AND FRENCH WORDS AND PHRASES AND ITS MEANING IN ANGLO-ASSAMESE

COMPILED & EDITED BY BASUMATARY

Made with ♥ on the Notion Press Platform
www.notionpress.com

Contents

I

A

ab ante (L) From before আগৰে পৰা।

ab extra (L) From without বাহিৰৰ পৰা।

ab initio (L) From the beginning আদিৰে পৰা।

ab intra (L) From within ভিতৰৰ পৰা।

ab ovo (L) From the egg, from the beginning গুৰিৰে পৰা।

ad extremum (L) To the extreme অতিকৈ।

ad finem (L) To the end শেহলৈকে।

ad infinitum (L) To infinity অশেষ অনন্ত কাললৈ।

ad interim (L) For the meantime ইতিমধ্যে, ইয়াৰ ভিতৰতে।

ad libitum (L) at pleasure ইচ্ছামতে।

ad litem (L) For a suit গোচৰৰ কাৰণে।

ad manum (L) at hand হাততে, প্ৰস্তুত।

ad modum (L) after the manner of সেইদৰে।

ad nauseam (L) To the pitch of causing disgust আমুৰাই যোৱাকৈ, পেট ওকট্-পাকট্ কৰাকৈ।

ad referendum (L) to be further considered পৰামৰ্শ কৰিব লগা, বিবেচনাধীন অৱস্থাত।

ad rem (L) To the purpose সেই অভিপ্ৰায়ে, সেই ভাবে।

ad valorem (L) According to value মূল্যমতে, টকাৰ পৰিমাণে।

ad verbum (L) Verbally মুখে মুখে।

ad vivum (L) to the life আজীৱন।

advocatus diaboil (L) A devil's advocate, an adverse critic কুতৰ্কীলোক, খুঁট ধৰি ফুৰোতা।

affaire d'amour (Fr) a love affair প্ৰেম বিষয়ক ঘটনা।

a fortiori (L) With stronger reason প্ৰবলতৰ যুক্তি-মতে।

a' la carte (Fr) According to the bill of fare খৰছৰ বিল মতে।

a la main (Fr) in hand, ready হাতত থকা, প্ৰস্তুত।

a' la mode (Fr) According to the custom দস্তুৰ-মতে।

Albion (L) An old name of Great Britain ইংলণ্ডৰ প্ৰাচীন নাম।

aliquando bonus dormital Homer us (L) Some time the good Homer nods কেতিয়াবা কেতিয়াবা মুনিৰো মতিভ্ৰম হয়।

alma mater (L) Bening mother আই মাতৃ (কোনো জনে পঢ়ি শুনি ওলাই যোৱা বিদ্যালয়)।

alter ego (L) A friend বন্ধু, প্ৰতিনিধি।

amour patriae (L) Love of country স্বদেশানুৰাগ।

amour vincit omnia (L) Love conquers all things মৰমে সকলোকে বশ কৰে।

anima mundi (L) The soul of the world জগতৰ সাৰ বস্তু।

anonyma (Gr) A showy woman of light fame, who is little known আঁতি গুৰি নোহোৱা ৰচকী তিৰোতা।

anno Domini (L) In the year of our Lord যীশুখ্ৰীষ্ট ওপজা বছৰৰ পৰা।

ante bellum (L) Before the war যুদ্ধৰ আগৰ।

ante meridiem (L) দুপৰৰ আগৰ, ১২ বজাৰ আগৰ। যেনে 12 a.m. ; before noon.

a paribus (L) From equals সমান সমানৰ পৰা।

apologia (Gr) An apologetic writing দোষ একৰাই ভালবি বোলাবলৈ লিখা কথা।

a' prima vista (It) at first sight পোণেই দেখাত।

a tout prix (Fr) At any price যিমান খৰচ হওক।

aqua (L) water পানী।

aqua vita (L) water of life, often applied to spirituous liquors ফটীকা।

aquila non capit mus cas (L) = an eagle does not catch flies সেন চৰায়ে মেহ মাখি নধৰে, ডাঙৰে সৰু কথাত মনে নিদিয়ে।

argumentum ad hominem (L) argument to the man,—that is to one's interests and passions কোনো ব্যক্তিৰ স্বাৰ্থ বা উদ্দেশ্য লৈ তৰ্ক।

argumentum ad ignorantiam (L) an argument based on ignorance of facts অজ্ঞতামূলক তৰ্ক।

argumentum ad rem (L) argument to the purpose মূল উদ্দেশ্যলৈ তৰ্ক বিতৰ্ক।

argumentum ad invidiam (L) argument appealing to low passions গালি সপনিপৰি কৰা তৰ্ক।

argumentum bacculinum (L) argument of the stick তৰ্ক কৰোঁতে কৰোঁতে মৰামৰি হোৱা তৰ্ক।

ariston metron (Gr) the middle course is the best মজলীয়া ভাবৰ উপায়েই ভাল উপায়।

audaces fortuna juvat (L) Fortune favours the daring সাহসী লোকেই লক্ষ্মীক লাভ কৰে।

auditque vocatus Apollo (L) ভক্তিতে দেবতাও বশ হয়।

au fond (Gr) At the bottom মূলত, গুৰিত।

au revoir (Fr) Adien সম্প্ৰতি বিদায়।

au royaume des aveugies les borgnes sont rois (Fr) in the kingdom of the blind the one eyed are the kings অন্ধকাৰ ৰাজ্যত এচকুৱাই ৰজা।

avante coureur (এভেণ্ট কুৰৰ্) **(Gr)** A forerunner অগ্ৰগামী।

a verbis ad verbera (L) From words to blows উতৰাউতৰিৰ পৰা মৰামৰি।

axioma medium (L) A generalisation from experience বহুত দেখি শুনি ধাৰ্য্য কৰা সাধাৰণ মত।

II

B

badaud (Fr) a simpleton ভেবা, ভেবুৰা মানুহ।

bagatelle (Gr) A trifle নিচেই সামান্য কথা।

barba tenus sapientes (L) sages in appearance only লোক দেখনীয়াৰ জ্ঞানী।

bal esprit (Fr) A person of genious প্ৰতিভাশালী লোক।

balle amie (Fr) a female friend সহচৰী।

beneficiaire (Fr) one receiving a benefit অনুগ্ৰহ বা সহায় পোৱা লোক।

bene qui latuit bene vixit (L) He has lived well who has lived obscure যেয়ে অজানিত-ভাবে আছে তেৱেঁই সুখে আছে।

bis dat qui cito bat (L) He who gives promptly,

gives twice যি ততালিকে দিয়ে সি দুগুণ দিয়াব সমান।

Bizarre (বিজেয়েৰ) *adj.* **(Fr)** eccentric grotesque অসভ্যালি, বলিয়ালি, উৎপতীয়া।

Blitz-krieg (ব্লিঝ-ক্রিগ্) *n.* vehement aeroplane attack, (Ger. *Krieg* war) উড়নীয় জাহাজব আক্রমণ (see under **War.**)

bona fides (L) Good faith সৰল বিশ্বাস।

bonhomic (Fr) Good nature সদ্ভাৱ; সৰলতা।

bonjour (বং-যুৰব) **(Fr)** good morning সু-প্ৰভাত।

borgen macht sorgen (Gr) Borrowing makes sorrowing ধাৰ কৰে যি শোকত পৰে সি।

III

C

Caeteris paribus (L) other things being equal আনবিলাক সমান হলে।

Cafe (Fr) A coffee-house কফি খোৱা দোকান।

Cantabit vacuns coram latrone viator (L) the empty traveller will sing before a robber মগনিয়াৰ পথিকৰ ডকাইতৰ কি ভয়।

Carpe diem (L) Seize the opportunity সুযোগ ল; পোৱা সুবিধা ভোগ কৰ।

Carteblanche (Fr) A blank sheet of paper full powers খালি কাগজ, পূৰা ক্ষমতা।

Causa sine quanon (L) an indispensable cause অপৰিহাৰ্য্য কাৰণ।

Centum (L) A hundred শত, এশ।

Conditio sine qua' non (L) an indispensable condition নহলে নোহোৱা বিধান।

Circuitus Verborum (L) a circumlocution বাগাড়ম্বৰ, বহুল কথা।

Cito (L) quickly তৎক্ষণাৎ।

Corpus delicti (L) The substance of the offence জগৰৰ সাৰ মৰ্ম্ম।

Coup de bonheur (কু-ডু-বং-ইউৰ) **(Fr)** stroke of good-luck ভাগ্যৰ ফেৰ।

Cucullus non facit monachum (L) The cowl does not make the monk উদাসীনৰ বেশ পিন্ধিলেই উদাস নহয়।

Contra bonos mores (L) against morals নীতি বিগৰ্হিত।

Coup de grace (Gr) A finishing stroke শেষ মাৰ্জ্জণ।

Coup de main (Fr) A sudden enterprise of effort হঠাৎ চেষ্টা, প্ৰধান উদ্যম, প্ৰথম হেঁচা।

Cul bono ? (L) For Whose benefit কাৰ উপকাৰৰ অৰ্থে ?

Cum grano salis (L) With a grain of salt,— i. e. with some allowance কিছু বাদ দি।

IV

D

d'accord (Fr) Agreed, in tune মিল।

da dextrom misero (L) Give the right hand to one who is miserable দুখীয়াক সহায় কৰা।

de bonne grace (Fr) with good grace willingly ইচ্ছাপূৰ্ব্বক, মৰমেৰে।

de gratia (L) By the grace of God ঈশ্বৰৰ অনুগ্ৰহত।

de-integro (L) Anew নকৈ।

dejeuner (Fr) Break-fast or lunch দিনৰ প্ৰথম আহাৰ।

de jure (L) In law, rightful আইন মতে, স্বত্ববান।

de-mal en pis (Fr) from bad to worse ক্ৰমে বেয়াতকৈ বেয়া।

demarche (Fr) A diplomatic measure শাসন কৌশল উপায়।

de mortuis nil nisi bonum (L) Say nothing but good of the dead মৃতকৰ ভালৰ বাজে বেয়া কব নেপায়।

de novo (L) Anew আকৌ নকৈ।

Deo gratias (L) Thanks to God ঈশ্বৰৰ প্ৰতি ধন্যবাদ।

detenu (Fr) or *(fem.)* **detenue (Fr)** A prisoner বন্দীয়াৰ, কাটকিয়াল, কয়েদী।

Deus avertat (L) God forbid ঈশ্বৰে নকৰোক।

Denus vobiscum (L) God be with you তোমাৰ ঈশ্বৰ সহায় হওক।

dictum sapienti sat est (L) A word to the

wise is enough জ্ঞানীৰ পক্ষে একেষাৰ কথাই বহুত।

Dieu et mon droit (F) God and my right ঈশ্বৰ আৰু মোৰ স্বত্ব।

di salto (It) At a leap একেজাপেই।

divide et impera (L) divide and rule বিপক্ষক ডাল ডাল কৰি শাসন কৰ।

dulce et decorum est pro patria mori (L) It is sweet and glorious to die for one's country স্বদেশৰ অৰ্থে প্ৰাণত্যাগ অতি সুন্দৰ আৰু গৌৰৱৰ কথা।

dum spiro spero (L) While I breathe I hope যিমান দিন শ্বাস সিমান দিন আশ।

dum vivimus vivamus (L) while we live let us live জীয়াই থকা কেদিন মানুহৰ দৰে থাকিব লাগে।

durante vita (L) during life জীৱিত অৱস্থাত।

V

E

e contra (L) contrarywise ওভোতা।

en ami (Fr) as a friend বন্ধুভাৱে।

en beau (Fr) As handsome অতি সুন্দৰ।

en masse (Fr) In a body জুমবান্ধি, আটাই বিলাক লগলাগি।

en passant (Fr) By the by এই প্ৰসঙ্গত, ইয়াৰ লগতে কবলগীয়া।

en route (Fr) On the road বাটত; let us go ব'লা।

entente cordiale (Fr) cordial understanding between two nations দুই ৰাজ্যৰ ভিতৰত সদ্ভাৱ, মিল।

e pluribus unum (L) one out of many বহুতৰ ভিতৰত এক।

e re nata (L) From the circumstances arisen সেই অৱস্থাৰ পৰা যিটো হৈছে।

errare est humanum (L) to err is human মানুহ মাত্ৰৰে ভুল হয়।

esse quam videri (L) To be rather than to seem বাহিৰে দেখুৱাতকৈ কাৰ্য্যত হব লাগে।

est modus in rebus (L) There is a proper mean in all things সকলো কথাৰে এটা মাধ্যম অৱস্থা আছে।

et ego in Arcadia (L) মयো আর্কেদিয়াত আছিলো অর্থাৎ আনে এই বিষয়ে যিমান জানে মযো সিমান জানো।

exempli gratia (L) e. g.=by way of example অর্থাৎ।

ex nature rei (L) from the nature of the case সেই কথাৰ অৱস্থা বুজি, কাৰ্য্যৰ গতিৰ পৰা।

ex nihilo nihili fit (L) Out of nothing, nothing comes য'ত একোৱেই নাই তাৰ পৰা একোতা উদ্ভৱ হ'ব নোৱাৰে।

ex officio (L) By virtue of his office কোনো কামত থকা গুণে হোৱা।

ex parte (L) On one side একতৰফা, বিপক্ষৰ অসাক্ষাতে।

ex re nata (L) According to circumstance that has arisen উপস্থিত ঘটনা অনুযায়।

VI

F

facile est inventis addere (L) It is easy to add to things invented already আনে যত্ন কৰি উলিওৱা বস্তুত জোৰা দিবলৈ বৰ সহজ।

facta non verbe (L) Deeds not words কাৰ্য্য (লাগে) কথা নহয়।

factum est (L) It is done এইটো কৰা হ'ল।

fait accompli (Fr) a thing already done আগেয়েই হৈ যোৱা কাম ; খাটাং কথা।

falsus is uno falsus in omnibus (L) false in one point false in all এটাত মিছা পৰিলে ই সকলোতে মিছা।

fama clamosa (L) a current scandal সকলোৰে জনাজাত বদনাম।

fas est et ab hoste doceri (L) It is right to be taught even by an enemy শত্ৰু হ'লেও তাৰ পৰা শিক্ষা লোৱা উচিত।

felicitas multos habet amicos (L) Prosperity has many friends সম্পদ কালত অনেক বন্ধু হয়।

felo de se (L) A suicide আত্মহত্যা।

femme savante (Fr) a learned woman শিক্ষিতা স্ত্ৰী।

feu de joie (Fr) a bonfire মেজি পুৰি কৰা জয়োৎসৱ।

fiat justitia ruat coelum (L) let justice be done though heaven falls স্বৰ্গ ভাগি পৰিলেও ন্যায্য পালন কৰিবা।

fide et amore (L) By faith and love বিশ্বাস আৰু স্নেহেৰে।

fide, sed cui vide (L) trust, but in whom take care বিশ্বাস কৰিবা, কিন্তু কেনে জনক কৰিবা সাৱধান হবা।

flecteri is nequeo superos Acherronta movebo (L) If I cannot move the gods I will stir up hell দেৱতাক লৰাব নোৱাৰিলেও নৰ্ককে ঘোদালিহে এৰিম; মাছ ধৰিব নোৱাৰিলেও পানী ঘোদলি কৰিম।

forte et fideli nihil difficile (L) To the brave and faithful nothing is difficult ধৰ্ম্মপৰায়ণ আৰু সাহসী জনৰ্ পক্ষে কোনো কথা অসাধ্য নহয়।

fraus pia (L) A pious fraud ধাৰ্ম্মিক ঠগী।

fronti nulla fides (L) No reliance on the face মুখ দেখি মানুহ চিনিব নোৱাৰি।

frou-frou (Fr) the rustling of women's clothes মাইকীৰ পোচাকৰ খচমচনি।

fugit hora (F) The hour flies সময় বৈ নেথাকে।

functus officio (L) out of office কামৰ পৰা অৱসৰ লৈ ওলাই অহা।

VII

G

gendermes (F) *n. pl.* Armed Police অস্ত্ৰধাৰী কনিষ্টবল বিলাক।

gens de condition (Fr) people of rank ডাঙৰ মানুহ, ধনী মানুহ।

gens de robe (Fr) lawyers উকীল সকল।

gravis ira regum est semper (L) the anger of kings is always serious ৰজাৰ খং অতি ভয়ঙ্কৰ।

gutta cavat lapidem (L) the drop wears away the stone পানী এটোপ এটোপকৈ পৰি শিলকো ক্ষয় কৰে।

VIII

H

heu pietas, heu prisca fides (L) Alas for piety ! alas for the ancient faith ! হায়! দয়াধৰ্ম্ম! হায়! পৌৰাণিক ধৰ্ম্ম-নিষ্ঠা।

hic et ubique (L) Here and every where ইয়াতো আন সকলো ঠাইতে, গোটেইখনতে।

hoc anno (L) In this year এই বছৰ।

hominibus plenum, amicis vacuum (L) Full of men, empty of friends মানুহ অসংখ্য কিন্তু বন্ধু শূন্য।

homme de fortune (Fr) Rich men ধনী লোক।

homo homini lupus (L) man is a wolf to man মানুহেই মানুহৰ শত্ৰু।

homo sum, humani nihil a me alienum puto (L) I am a man, I count nothing human indifferent to me মই এটা মানুহ যেতিয়া, মানুহ কোনো প্ৰকাৰে মোৰ শত্ৰু হব নোৱাৰে।

homo unius libri (L) A man of one book এটা মাত্ৰ কিতাপ পঢ়া লোক, অশিক্ষিত।

honi soit qui mal y pense (Fr) The shame be his who thinks ill of it যি ভাৱে মন্দ ভাৱে হওক দণ্ড।

honneur et patrie (Fr) Honour and native land সন্মান আৰু স্বদেশ।

honores mutant mores (L) honours change manners সন্মান পালে মানুহৰ আচৰণ বদলে।

hostis honori invidia (L) An enemy's hatred is an honour শত্ৰুৰ ঘৃণা সন্মান সূচক।

humanum est errare (L) to err is human মানুহ মাত্ৰৰে ভুল হয়।

IX

I

ibidem (L) In the same place, thing or case তাতে।

idem (L) The same সেয়ে।

id est (L) i. e. That is অৰ্থাৎ।

ignoratio elenchi (L) The fallacy of ignoring the main point (তৰ্ক শাস্ত্ৰমতে) মূল কথা এৰি বগাই ফুৰা (দোষ)।

ignoratio legis neminem excusat (L) Ignorance of the law excuses no body দোষ কৰি আইন নেজানো বুলিয়েই কোনো সাৰিব নোৱাৰে।

il penseroso (L) The pensive man চিন্তাশীল লোক।

impasse (L) An insoluble difficulty বিমোৰ সঙ্কট।

impedimenta (L) luggage মাল-বস্তু।

imperium in imperio (L) a government within government এক শাসন প্ৰণালীৰ ভিতৰতে আন এটা শাসন প্ৰণালী, ওপৰা-উপৰি গৱৰ্ণমেণ্ট।

in esse (L) in fact আচলতে, হওঁতে।

in extenso (L) extensively বিস্তাৰিত ৰূপে।

in flagranti delicto (L) In the very act of committing the crime জগৰ কৰি থাকোঁতেই হাতে হাতে ধৰা।

in memoriam (L) In memory স্মৰণাৰ্থে।

in re (L) In the matter সেই বিষয়ে।

in situ (L) In the original situation প্ৰথম অৱস্থাত, পূৰ্ব্বৰ ঠাইতে।

in stain quo (L) In the former state আগৰ অৱস্থাত।

inter alia (L) Among other things আন বিলাকৰ মাজত, মাজতে।

inter arma silent legis (L) যুদ্ধৰ মাজত আইন-কানুন নচলে।

inter nose (L) Between ourselves আমাৰ ভিতৰত।

inter se (L) Amongst themselves সিহঁতৰ ভিতৰত।

in toto (L) Entirely সম্পূৰ্ণৰূপে, সমূলি।

intra muros (L) Within the walls ভিতৰুৱা; ঘৰৰ ভিতৰৰ।

in transitu (L) On the passage গৈ থাকোতে, বাটত নিওঁতে।

ipse dexit (L) He himself said it তাৰ নিজৰ কথাতে; resting on bare authority.

ipso facto (L) Virtually ফলত, পৰিণামে।

ira furor brevis est (L) rage is a madness in short খং বা কোপ এটা খন্তেকীয়া বলিয়ালি।

X

J

judex damnatur cum nocens absolvetur (L) the judge is blamed when a guilty man is acquited দোষীয়ে দণ্ড নেপালে জজক গ্লানি কৰে।

jure divino (L) By divine law ঐশ্বৰিক বিধান মতে।

jure humano (L) by man made law মানুহে কৰা বিধান মতে।

XI

L

labour ipse voluptas (L) Labour itself is pleasure পৰিশ্ৰম মাত্ৰই সন্তোষজনক।

l'allegro (L) The cheerful man আনন্দময় লোক।

l'apsus calami (L) A slip of the pen লেখোঁতে ভুল।

l'apsus linguae (L) A slip of the tongue কথাৰ কোবত ওলোৱা ভুল কথা।

l'apsus memoriae (L) A slip of the memory পাহৰণ।

lingua franca (It) any mixed jargon দোৱান, বুজিব নোৱৰা কথা।

locum tenens (L) A deputy or substitue প্ৰতিনিধি, বদলি।

locus standi (L) A place for standing, a right to interfere, স্থিতি, থিয় হবৰ ঠাই, হস্তক্ষেপ কৰিবৰ অধিকাৰ।

lusus naturae (L) A freak of nature প্ৰকৃতিৰ ধেমালি, ঈশ্বৰ খেলা।

XII

M

magni nominis umbra **(L)** The mere shadow of a mighty name মহৎ লোকৰ নামৰ ছাঁটোৰেই।

magnum bonum **(L)** a great good অতি মঙ্গল কার্য্য।

mala fide **(L)** Trecherously বিশ্বাসঘাতকতা কৰি, অসৎ ভাবে।

mulgre nou **(Fr)** In spite of us আমাৰ হিংসাত।

matinee **(Fr)** A morning performance দিনৰ ভাৱনা বা গান বাজনা।

mea culpa (L) By my own fault মোৰ নিজৰ দোষত।

melee (Fr) A confused scuffle হুৰামুৰা।

meo periculo (L) At my own risk মোৰ নিজৰ দায়িত্বত।

modus operandi (L) mode of operation কামৰ বেহা।

modus vivendi (L) mode of living জীৱিকাৰ উপায়।

monsieur (Fr.) Sir, Mr.—*pl.* **messieurs** মহাশয়, ডাঙ্গৰীয়া।

more majorum (L) After the manner of our ancestors আমাৰ পূৰ্ব্ব পুৰুষৰ দস্তুৰমতে।

motu propreo (L) Of his own accord স্বেচ্ছা-পূৰ্ব্বক।

mutatis mutandis (L) with necessary changes সালসলনি কৰি।

mutuus consensus (L) Mutual consent পৰস্পৰৰ সন্মতিক্ৰমে।

XIII

N

ne. cede malis (L) Yield not to misfortune বিপদত অধৈৰ্য্য নহবা।

necessitas non habet legem (L) Necessity has no law আপদত অযুগুত।

nem con (L) Without opposition কোনো আপত্তি নোহোৱাকৈ, বিনা ওজৰে।

ne plus ultra (L) Nothing further অত্যুৎকৃষ্ট, ইয়াতকৈ আৰু বেচি একো নাই।

ne sutor ultra crepidam (L) Let not the cobbler go beyond his last যি যেনে অৱস্থাৰ মানুহ তাক তাতে থাকিবলৈ দিব লাগে।

nihil ad rem (L) Nothing to the point আচল বিষয়ত একো নহয়।

nil admirari (L) To admire nothing লোকৰ একোকে ভাল নেদেখা, আত্মম্ভৰী।

nil admirari (L) To admire nothing লোকৰ একোকে ভাল নেদেখা, আত্মম্ভৰী।

nil desperandum (L) Never despair কেতিয়াও হতাশ নহবা।

nisi Dominus frustra (L) Unless the Lord favours everything is vain ঈশ্বৰে নকৰালে সকলো মিছা।

nisi prius (L) Unless previously আগতে নহলে।

nolens volens (L) Whether he will or not সি ইচ্ছা কৰোক নকৰোক।

non compos mentis (L) not of sound mind মন ঠিক নথকা, বিভ্ৰম।

non vivimus edere, sed edimus vivere (L) We do not live to eat, but eat to live আমি খাবলৈ জীয়াই থকা নাই কিন্তু জীয়াই থাকিবলৈহে খাওঁ।

nota bene (L) N. B., Mark well বিশেষকৈ জানিব লগা।

XIV

O

obiter dictum (L) A cursory remark কথাৰ প্ৰসঙ্গত কোৱা কোনো কথা।

omne ignotum pro magnifico (L) everything unknown is considered to be magnificent নেদেখা বস্তুটো বৰ ডাঙ্গৰ বুলি ভাব হয়।

omnia vincit amor (L) love conquer everything মৰমে সকলোকে বশ কৰে।

on dit (Fr) A flying rumour উড়া বাতৰি, ৰৌঢ়ি।

O tempora ! O more ! (L) What sad times ! what dreadful doings ! হায়! কি সাংঘাটিক দিন, কি সাংঘাটিক কাৰ্য্য।

otia dant vitia (L) idleness begets vice এলাহে পাপ জন্মাই, এলেহুৱা হৈ বহি থাকিলে মানুহৰ কু-ভাবনা উৎপত্তি হয়।

XV

P

pactum illicitum (L) An illegal compact অবৈধ সম্মিলন, অন্যায় বন্ধবস্তু।

par excellence (Fr) Eminently আদৰ্শ স্বৰূপে।

pari passu (Fr) what equal pace together একেলগে, সমানে।

per fas et nefas (L) Through right and wrong ন্যায় অন্যায় একো নগণি।

personnel (Fr) Persons employed in any service কোনো কামত খটা লোক সকল; কৰ্ম্মকাৰকবিলাক।

pleno jure (Fr) with full authority পুৰা ক্ষমতাৰে।

pot hoc (L) After this ইয়াৰ পাচত।

pot mortem (L) After death মৰাৰ পাচত।

prima facie (L) On the first view প্ৰথমে দেখাত।

primo (L) In the first place প্ৰথমতে, আদিতে।

pro patria (L) For our country স্বদেশৰ বাবে।

pro re nata (L) For a special emergency কোনো বিশেষ দৰকাৰৰ বাবে।

pro tanto (L) For so much ইমানৰ বাবে।

pro tempore (L) For the time being অলপ দিনৰ নিমিত্তে।

XVI

Q

quoere (L) Inquire সোধা।

qui tacet consentit (L) who keeps silence consents মৌনে সম্মতি লক্ষণম, নেমাতি থাকিলেই সম্মতি বুজায়।

qui va la ? (Fr) Who goes there সেইটো কোন গৈছে ?

quod erat demonstrandum (L) or **Q. E. D.** Which was to be proved প্ৰমাণ কৰি দেখুৱাব লাগে।

quod vide (L) Which see সেইটো চোৱা।

quo jure ? (L) By what right কোনো স্বত্ব মতে।

XVII

R

rara avis (L) A rare bird, prodigy অদ্ভুত জন্তু।

religio loci (L) The religious spirits of the place সেই ঠাইৰ ধৰ্ম্মভাৱ।

repondenz sil vous plait (ৰেচ্-পংস্থে-চিল্-ভোঁ-প্লে) **(Fr) R. S. V. P.**=Reply if you please অনুগ্ৰহ কৰি উত্তৰ দিব।

ruit mole sua (L) It falls by its own weight ইয়াৰ নিজৰ ভৰতে নিজে পৰিছে।

rué contre ruse (L) cunning against cunning হুলে হুলক কাঢ়ে; টেঙ্গৰে টেঙ্গৰে লাগ।

XVIII

S

salvo jure (L) The right being safe স্বত্ব নিৰাপদ হোৱাত।

sans gene (Fr) at ease বিনা বাধাই।

sans souci (Fr) Without care বিনাযত্নে।

Sapere aude (L) Dare to be wise জ্ঞান প্ৰকাশ কৰিবলৈ সাহস কৰিবা।

sat sapienti (L) enough for the wise জ্ঞানীৰ নিমিত্তে সেয়ে বহুত।

sic itur ad astra (L) such is the way to the stars to fame তৰাৰ ওচৰ চাপিবলৈ এয়ে বাট; যশ লাভ কৰিবৰ এয়ে উপায়।

similia similibus curantur (L) like things are cured by like যেয়ে ৰোগ জন্মাই সেয়ে তাৰ ঔষধ, হুলে হুলক কাঢ়ে।

si vis pacem para bellum (L) If you would have peace, be ready for war শান্তি লাগে যদি যুদ্ধলৈ সাজু হোৱা।

status quo (L) The state in which তেনে অৱস্থাত, স্থিতি, প্ৰতিপত্তি।

Sturm und Drang (Ger) storm and stress, violent commotion জোৰজবৰ, খুন্দা, হেঁচা।

sub judice (L) Under consideration বিচাৰা-ধীন।

sub poena (L) under a penalty দণ্ডযোগ্য, দণ্ডভোগ কৰি।

sub rosa (L) Privately গোপনে।

summum bonum (L) The chief good শ্ৰেষ্ঠ সুখ।

Sutor ne supra crepidam judicaret (L) let not the cobbler venture his last ফটা জোঁতা সিয়া মুচীয়াৰক তাৰ ঠাঁচ এৰি ওপৰলৈ উধাব নিদিবা; ছোট মানুহক ডাঙৰটো কাৰ্য নুতুলিবা।

XIX

T

Teadium vitae (L) Weariness of life জীৱনৰ অশান্তি।

tempora mutantur, nos et mutamur in illis (L) Time are changed and we with them সময় পৰিবৰ্তনশীল আমিও তাৰ লগতে তেনে।

tempus fugit (L) Time flies সময় উড়ি উড়ি গৈছে।

terra incognita (L) an unknown country অপৰিচিত দেশ।

tertium quid (L) A third something কোনো তৃতীয়।

timeo Danaos et dona ferentes (L) I fear the Greeks even when bringing gifts গ্ৰীক্‌-বিলাক এনে ভয় লগা যে সিহঁতে পুৰস্কাৰ আনিলেও ভয় নকৰাকৈ নেথাকিবা।

tria juncta in uno (L) three in one এজনতে তিনি জন, এজনতে তিনি মূৰ্ত্তি।

Tycoon (টাইকুন্) *n.* **(Jap)** the **Shoguns** of Japan জাপান দেশৰ সেনাপতি; great prince ডাঙৰ কোঁৱৰ।

XX

U

ultra vires (L) Beyond one's power ক্ষমতাৰ বহিৰ্ভূত।

ultima thule (L) The utmost limit নিচেই শেষ সীমা।

ut infra (L) As below তলত কোৱা মতে।

ut supra (L) As above ওপৰত কোৱা মতে, ওপৰোক্ত।

XXI

V

vade mecum (L) A constant companion নিত্য সহচৰ, লগত লৈ ফুৰুৱা।

valet de chambre (Fr) An attendant লগুৱা।

veni, vidi, vici (L) I came, I saw, I conquered মই আহিলো, দেখিলো, জয় কৰিলো।

berbatim et literatim (L) word for word and letter for letter প্ৰতি আখৰে আখৰে শব্দে শব্দে।

verbum sapienti sat est (L)=*verb sap* and *verb. sat.* A word is enough for a wise man জ্ঞানীৰ নিমিত্তে একেবাৰেই বহুত।

veritas odium parti (L) Truth begets hatred সঁচা কথাই ঘৃণা জন্মাব।

versus or V. (L) Against বনামে, বিপক্ষে।

vestigia nulla retrorsum (L) No going back (from lion's den) সিংহৰ গাঁতৰ পৰা উভতি অহা টান।

via (L) By way of বাটেদি।

via media (L) a middle course মজামজি উপায়।

via trita, via tuta The beaten path is the safe path চলাচল কৰি থকা পথেই সুপথ।

vice (L) in the place or কাৰো ঠাইত।

vice versa (L) The terms being exchanged আকৌ ইটোৰ পৰা সিটোলৈ, অদল-বদলকৈ।

vis a tergo (L) comulsion from behind পাচফালৰ পৰা দিয়া হেঁচা।

vis a vis (Fr) Opposite মুখামুখী, বিপৰীতে।

vita patris (L) In the fathers life time পিতাৰ দিনত। (or V. P.)

vivat regina (L) Long live the queen ৰানী দীৰ্ঘায়ু হওক।

vivat rex (L) Long live the king ৰজা দীৰ্ঘায়ু হওক।

viva voce (L) By oral testimony মুখে মুখে লোৱা। মৌখিক প্ৰমাণ দ্বাৰা।

vive valeque (L) life and health to you তোমাৰ আয়ুৰ শ্ৰীবৃদ্ধি হওক।

volo non valeo (L) I am willing but unable মই ইচ্ছা কৰো কিন্তু নোৱাৰো।

Vox populi vox Dei (L) the voice of the people is the voice of God ৰাইজৰ মতেই ঈশ্বৰৰ মত।

Vulgo (L) commonly সাধাৰণতে।

XXII

W

Weltschmerz (Ger) sympathy with world sorrow পৃথিৱীৰ লোকৰ দুখত দুঃখিত হোৱা গুণ।

Weltgeist (Ger) the world spirit সংসাৰৰ উত্তেজনা।

XXIII

Z

Zombie (ঝম্‌বি) *n.* bodies without soul, a dead man with seeming life, (in **Haiti** isle) জীবাত্মাহীন লোক, প্রেত।

Printed by Libri Plureos GmbH in Hamburg,
Germany

9 798889 752608